THE UNCOMMON FEAST

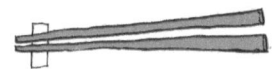

By the same author:
Burning Rice
Peony
Painting Red Orchids
Another Language
Rainforest

THE UNCOMMON FEAST

ESSAYS, POEMS, AND RECIPES

EILEEN CHONG

RECENT
WORK
PRESS

The Uncommon Feast
Recent Work Press
Canberra, Australia

Copyright © Eileen Chong, 2018

ISBN: 9780648087892 (paperback)

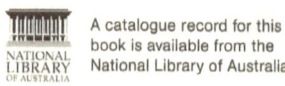 A catalogue record for this book is available from the National Library of Australia

All rights reserved. This book is copyright. Except for private study, research, criticism or reviews as permitted under the Copyright Act, no part of this book may be reproduced, stored in a retrieval system, or transmitted in any form by any means without prior written permission. Enquiries should be addressed to the publisher.

Cover and interior illustrations: © Colin Cassidy 2018
Cover design: Colin Cassidy
Author photograph: Charlene Winfred Photography

recentworkpress.com

For my grandparents, who fed my parents, and for my parents, who fed me in turn, and taught me to how to feed others well.

CONTENTS

Introduction by Judith Beveridge

The Common Table	1
Diana's Hainanese Chicken Rice	6
Eating and Telling: A Personal Food History	15
Burning Rice	22
Mid-Autumn Mooncakes	23
Grandmother's Dish	26
Chinese Ginseng	28
Cleansing Ritual	31
Chinese Ginseng Chicken Soup	30
Evensong	32
Father, Crow	34
Eating Durian	36
August, Pomelo	37
Pomelo, Pork and Prawn Salad	38
The Task	41
Singapore Chilli Crab	43
Kumera	45
Cooking for One	46
Rice-Dumplings	47
Ash, Wednesday	49
Sun Ming Restaurant, Parramatta	51
Xiao Long Bao (Little Dragon Dumplings)	53
Lord Nelson	55
Crossing the Spey	57
A Winter's Night	59
Eileen's Scotch Broth	61
Afterword	64

INTRODUCTION

The poet William Carlos Williams famously said: '*It is difficult to get the news from poems,* yet *men die miserably every day for lack of what is found there.*' Here, the link between poetry and food, or poetry *as* food is very clear. Poetry and food are not commonly thought of together, at least not in most households, but in *The Uncommon Feast* Eileen Chong brings them into a most potent relationship. The dishes and meals that her poems evoke remind us of poetry's ability also to be bread on the table, a place where both intimacy and communion can be shared just as much as a home-cooked meal.

You could argue that a good poem and a good recipe have much in common. Both need to be very precise, no extraneous ingredients, all the weights and measures, the words and the lines must all have as their purpose the final result. A poem, like a well-executed recipe, becomes more than just the sum of its parts. A successful recipe comes about through much testing, by trial and error, just as a poem must undergo a number of drafts before it is perfected. Both a meal and a poem come to us orally, a poet will test the words in the mouth just as a cook tastes how the flavours are developing and advancing. The principal functions of a well-cooked meal are much the same as those of a well-written poem: as a form of communication, as a social and cultural contract between certain group members, as an expression of love and intimacy, of sustenance and shared values, as a record of fleeting, transient moments, as a repository for memories, as an enactment of ritual.

The poems in *The Uncommon Feast* are not simply listings of culinary expertise and delights, they are above all explorations of relationships in their many manifestations. There are meals between lovers, friends, family members, and all are beautifully nuanced; there is the joy of shared cooking, the complications of getting a meal right, the medicinal uses of certain foods, the use of food as emotional currency, and the joy of eating alone. These poems are full of sensation and sensuality, and while they emphasise that adage 'we are what we eat', they also clearly point out that we are more importantly made by culture and language, the words we possess and the words that possess us. As Paul Kane has written in his introduction to Eileen Chong's US publication, *Another Language,* 'It was Roland Barthes who taught us to regard cuisine as a semiotic system, a language with a grammar and Chong uses it—speaks that language—to articulate cultural difference, yes, but also to register and record the actual ingredients of her life, to give us a taste of it.'

As well as the poems there are finely orchestrated prose pieces, recipes and illustrations by Colin Cassidy. But it is the poems which are at the heart of this book, they are the main course with their own authentic emotional seasonings.

Judith Beveridge

THE COMMON TABLE

My maternal grandmother, the last of my grandparents, celebrated her 85th birthday yesterday. I watch on a video screen as she eats her breakfast long-life noodles. The boiled egg left whole: an embryo, the universe, the beginning and the end. I surprise myself by thinking and speaking in Hokkien. I don't speak this language to anyone else. I have not spoken in this tongue since the last time I saw her, months ago, in Singapore.

My grandmother has dementia. She asks me why I am not there. I tell her I am working. Work is always a valid excuse. Work comes before family; without work there is no family. She asks me what work I do. I tell her I write books, I read books, I teach books. She understands only the last. She asks again, *What work you do?* I tell her, *Books*. She says, *Oh, you teach books, that's right*.

She passes the phone to my mother. It is the first time we have spoken in weeks, though we have texted. My parents have been travelling. She wants to know how the Prime Minister's Literary Awards ceremony went. I tell her *I was the only Asian in the room*. She tells me she is proud of me. *Try harder*, she says. 'Try harder' is a catchphrase I have heard all my life. 'Better luck next time,' 'bad luck', 'too bad'. Ours is a family that tries harder. Ours is a culture that believes in better luck, next time.

I spoke to my father's mother in the months before she died, years ago, my eldest uncle translating. As her story progressed, his translation became more skeletal. What I gathered: my grandmother had been a child bride, married off in poverty to another family in the village. She begged her mother to let her return home. *No, for shame.* Within the month, my grandmother, aged 16, with the help of her brothers, scaled a village wall and boarded a boat bound for Malaysia. I didn't speak Hakka, and still don't. There are so many gaps in this story.

When I was nine, I would accompany my mother's mother during the school holidays to various homes of her friends' where she would play mahjong. She was a formidable player who would gamble all day. I would bring books with me to fill the hours. She wasn't happy with me. *Books, books, books*—a homophone for *lose* in Mandarin. Her worker's hands sweeping over the restless tiles.

Both my grandmothers were illiterate. My paternal grandmother's father was a doctor; my maternal grandmother's father ran a dry goods store. Both these educated men kept their daughters from school, from bigger things in life. How to tell my grandmother I write for a living?

I see my psychologist the week before the prize is announced. She tells me to shop for a new dress. She tells me I have already won. But in my world, winning is not winning until you have won completely. I smile a lot at the event. I am happy to be there. I am proud to be standing with my fellow poets. They don't see colour. I am seated at lunch, and I realise I don't see colour, either. I am the only person of colour seated in this room.

I go for a walk. In the gardens of Parliament House, I see two men in chef's whites on their smoke break. They are Chinese. I stop in the bathroom. It is shut for cleaning. I call out and ask where the nearest open bathroom is. The cleaner comes out, smiling, and directs me down the hallway. She, too, is Asian. I head back to lunch. I sit down again, and a waiter comes up and offers me a drink. I look up. His name-tag says 'Edward'. I tell him, *Edward, we are the only Asians in this room*. He says, *Well, there's another one of us, but she's just finished her shift*. We smile at each other. He moves on to serve someone else.

So, my people are here—invisible, but present. I feel like a fraud: sitting down to lunch, being served. The poets are at another table. I make literary small talk with a historian. I ask him how he became a writer. He says he was born into a family of writers. The publisher to my right is puzzled when I tell her my publisher is not my editor; that I edit my own work, mostly. I cannot tell if she is puzzled because it is different for writers who aren't poets, or because of how I look. I am embarrassed that I even think this.

I tell someone I admire how much I like his work. He returns the compliment by telling me that many of my poems are like recipes, and if I collected them into a book, I might have some success with it. I am speechless. I feel put in my place, and ashamed. I return to my table. My husband is sitting there, waiting for me.

My husband is six feet tall, with ash-blonde hair and blue eyes. He looks particularly dashing today in a suit. People detect his faint Scottish accent and almost always want to ask him about it. When we turned up at the doors of Parliament House, I asked the security guard where to go for the event. He gave the answer to my husband. A woman just inside the doors was checking names off a list. She asked for our names, looking at my husband. When we went to the counter to pick up our security passes, the officer asked which shortlist category my husband was in. Later, as we walked away from the desk, my husband and I exchanged meaningful looks. He said, *It's the suit.* But we both know better. Later, we perfect the script. When someone speaks to him, he says, loudly and proudly, *Eileen has shortlisted for poetry. I'm the handbag.*

It is a relief when my name was pronounced correctly at the award announcements; I had raised it with the organisers prior to the event. I was brought up with my name pronounced 'Ee-leen', as an Anglicisation of my Chinese name, Yilin. For years I answered to 'Ai-leen'—*it's an Irish name, your name is Ei-leen*. It was easier not to fight. The name of my book was mispronounced as *Painting Red Orchards*. I quite like the notion of red orchards; rows of trees teeming with fruit, glossy, heavy, ready for harvest.

Some months ago, my mother held a cooking class at her community centre in Sydney. She wanted to teach her students how to cook Hainanese chicken rice and asked me to help her with the recipe. I told her to write it in as much detail as she could, and then I would edit it. She came over one afternoon and I opened up my laptop, ready to type. She handed me her notes. They were indecipherable. I had never asked to read anything my mother had written before. This was going to take some time.

My mother does not understand what I do for a living. She has never read any of my books. She has attended some of my readings, but we don't discuss my poems. She tells me I look good on stage. On Saturdays, when I buy flowers and arrange them in a vase, she tells me I should be a florist. When I colour her hair in the laundry sink, she says that I could be a hairdresser. These are real jobs, involving real work.

We are sitting at my kitchen table. I ask my mother for an equipment list and an ingredient list. Then we start to cook. Step-by-step, she tells me what she is doing, and I put words to it. She mimes lifting a chicken out of hot stock. I ask her what she is using, her hands? She laughs. We settle on *tongs*. She moves her hand in a circular fashion over an imaginary chicken. I say *drizzle*. Two hours later, we have her recipe. I print it out, and title it: *Diana's Hainanese Chicken Rice*. She is shy at our creation. She holds the recipe in her hands, and reads it. She looks up and says to me, *You are a writer.*

The historian at my table asked me how I became a writer. I tell him both my grandmothers were illiterate. That I didn't grow up with books in the house. That no one read to me when I was a child. That I taught myself to read when I was six. I was sitting on the floor, turning the pages of a library book, and the meaning of the words started to surface—the story was about a monkey in a tree. I was born in the year of the monkey.

I climbed up to the kitchen shelves where my mother's cookbooks were. I started to read: I pored over all the beautiful photographs of food, all the precise measurements and methods. By the time I went to primary school, I knew the difference between *boil, poach, bake, fry, grill*. Fry is what my maternal grandmother did to noodles at a hawker stall in Albert Complex in Singapore. She cooked fried Hokkien prawn noodles for paying customers at $1 a plate, and put six children through school; three went to university, including my auntie. My eldest uncle has a PhD.

In the kitchen in my apartment in Sydney, there is a photograph of my grandmother smiling down at me, eating the fried Hokkien prawn noodles I cooked for her from her recipe. Some of my poems might look like recipes, because my first words were gleaned from the need for nourishment, from the obsession over how to feed a family, how to keep them clothed, safe, and warm. I am safe, warm, and fed. I am writing, and I am seated at the table. My people exist. You know who we are. Look at us. Speak with us. Listen to us. We are one, and we are many. Let us feast together.

DIANA'S HAINANESE CHICKEN RICE

There are several components to this dish, namely:
1. stock,
2. chicken,
3. flavoured rice,
4. chilli sauce, and
5. a garnish.

The ingredients and method are listed for each component.

You will need a:
- deep pot to hold enough liquid to immerse a whole chicken in it,
- large bowl or pot that will hold enough iced water to immerse a whole cooked chicken,
- heat-resistant strainer or colander,
- large pair of tongs,
- frying pan,
- rice cooker, and
- blender.

To serve:
- large serving plate
- rice bowls or smaller plates
- sauce dishes
- soup bowls

1. STOCK

Ingredients:

Two chicken frames / carcasses

One thumb-sized piece of fresh ginger, peeled and sliced

One whole garlic bulb, cloves separated and peeled but left whole

3 litres of cold water

Salt to taste

Pepper to taste

Method:

Place all ingredients into a large, deep stock pot.

Bring to boil over high heat.

Lower the heat to a simmer, with the pot uncovered.

Skim the scum off the top of the stock repeatedly until clear, about half an hour.

Strain and reserve the liquid from the pot. Discard all solids.

Pour the stock back into the pot and bring to a boil again.

Lower the heat to a simmer again, with the pot uncovered

2. CHICKEN

Ingredients:

One medium whole chicken with skin on (about 1.6kg)

One thumb-sized piece of fresh ginger, peeled and sliced

Simmering stock (from above) in pot

Two litres of ice-cold water in deep bowl or pot

One tablespoon of sesame oil

One tablespoon of light soy sauce

Method:

Rinse the chicken inside and out, well.

Remove the fat at the tail of the chicken (parson's nose). Reserve for chilli component.

Lower the entire bird into the simmering stock, breast side up. (Chicken will float.)

Ensure the stock continues to simmer gently on low heat.

After 5 minutes, turn the chicken breast side down in the liquid.

Continue to simmer for 5 minutes.

Chicken will not be fully cooked at this stage.

Very carefully, remove the chicken from the stock with a large pair of tongs, making sure all liquid from the cavity drains back into the stock. Be sure to keep the chicken whole.

Keep the stock on a simmer.

SUBMERGE THE ENTIRE BIRD

Immediately transfer chicken to bowl or pot with ice-cold water.

Submerge the entire bird, rotating it several times to ensure the temperature of the bird is lowered. (This is to ensure the formation of gelatin, which makes the flesh of the chicken very smooth.)

Transfer the (now cool) chicken back into the hot stock, breast side up, ensuring it continues to simmer, for another 10 minutes.

Rotate the chicken breast-side down, and simmer for another 10 minutes.

Remove chicken from the stock with a large pair of tongs, making sure all liquid from the cavity drains back into the stock.

Reserve the stock, but turn the heat off.

Place chicken on a plate or a cutting board to rest.

Check the chicken for doneness by piercing the flesh at the junction of the thigh. If the liquid runs clear, the chicken is cooked. Alternatively, test the temperature of the bird with a meat thermometer.

If the chicken is not cooked, return to the hot stock and simmer again for 5 to 10 more minutes as required.

When the chicken is cooked, rub the entire bird, in and out, with the sesame oil.

Then rub the entire bird, in and out, with the light soy sauce.

Leave the chicken to rest, uncovered.

3. FLAVOURED RICE

Ingredients:

4 cups of uncooked jasmine rice, rinsed

8 cups of chicken stock

Rice cooker

One thumb-sized piece of ginger, peeled and sliced

One teaspoon of sesame oil

One teaspoon of salt

Method:

Add stock to rice, and cook rice in rice cooker. When cooked, keep warm.

If you do not have a rice cooker, add uncooked rice to stock in a non-stick saucepan.

Cover and bring to a boil.

Uncover and lower to a simmer.

Allow liquid to evaporate and rice to be fully cooked.

Keep warm.

4. CHILLI SAUCE

Ingredients:

Chicken fat from tail (previously reserved from chicken)

8 chillies (long red), cut stems off

Thumb-sized piece of ginger, peeled and left whole

6 cloves of garlic, peeled and left whole

The juice of one green lime, or lemon

Pinch of salt

1 teaspoon of sugar

Frying pan

Blender

Method:

In a hot frying pan, render the chicken fat until liquid. Discard any solids, and reserve the liquid.

Place all other ingredients into the blender

Blend in bursts, until a smooth paste is formed.

Add the liquid chicken fat and blend until smooth.

5. GARNISH

1 tomato, sliced thinly

1 small continental cucumber, unpeeled, sliced thinly

1 small bunch of coriander, leaves and stems, roughly chopped

1 teaspoon sesame oil

1 teaspoon of light soy sauce

1 tablespoon of kecap manis (sweet dark soy sauce)

HOW TO SERVE:

With a cleaver, carve the chicken into parts. Diana will demonstrate.

It is your choice whether you leave the skin and bones intact.

The meat on the thighs and breasts should be sliced.

The wings and the drumsticks can be left whole.

On a large plate, place the sliced cucumber and tomato in the middle in thin layers.

Arrange the carved chicken on top of the cucumber and tomatoes.

Drizzle the chicken with the sesame oil and light soy sauce.

Arrange the coriander on top of the chicken.

Place chicken in the middle; this is for sharing.

Serve the hot, flavoured rice in rice bowls or plates.

Serve a portion of hot soup on the side (you can garnish it with coriander and/or spring onion).

Serve the chilli sauce in sauce dishes, along with the kecap manis if desired.

EATING AND TELLING:
A PERSONAL FOOD HISTORY

I grew up in Singapore in the 1980s. Recess break at school was about rushing to the tuckshop and joining the queue for one of five or six food stalls. Here's what I remember, nearly thirty years later.

There was the hot soup lady: you picked your noodle (*mee*—yellow Hokkien noodles, *mee kia*—thin egg noodles, *mee pok*—flat egg noodles, *bee hoon*—thin rice vermicelli, *kway teow*—flat rice noodles, or a mix), whether you wanted it in soup, or dry with a sauce. The basic noodle dish, at fifty cents, came with several slices of fishcake and two fishballs. You could add fresh vegetables (*chye sim*—one of my friends got a bonus live caterpillar with her vegetables once, or *tau gay*—beansprouts), more fishballs, or even pork meatballs (Chinese-style, factory-made, bound with flour). An order would sound like this: "Fifty cent yellow noodle soup", or "dry bee hoon no chilli add *tau gay*".

There was the rice stall, where you picked servings of pre-cooked dishes to go with a serving of rice. Examples of these dishes would be fried eggs, steamed eggs, stir-fried vegetables, sweet and sour pork, pork slices stir-fried with spring onions and ginger, deep fried chicken wings... You pointed at the dishes, your selections would be put on a plate with rice, and the cost would be added up depending on what you ordered. Meat dishes cost more than vegetable dishes. If you charmed the uncle or auntie (respectful terms for adult males and females), they would give you more at the same price. I rarely ate at this stall, because the food was too similar to what I would eat for dinner at home.

The snack stall sold savoury snacks such as steamed tapioca cakes, hot dogs in soft buns, and what was to be my entry into spicy food, *otak otak*, a spiced fish paste sealed into *attap* leaves and grilled over charcoal. There was a 'white', non-spicy variety that I usually ordered. One day, the auntie made a mistake and gave me a spicy one. I was

too hungry or embarrassed to return it, and ate it. I never bought the non-spicy version again.

The Muslim food stall served dishes such as *mee rebus* (a wonderful Chinese-Malay hybrid dish consisting of thick yellow noodles in a gravy made with sweet potato and *tau-cheung*—fermented beans, topped with fried cubes of beancurd, beansprouts and a sliver of boiled egg, which the *Makcik* would magically cut with a fishing line), *mee siam* (another hybrid dish of rice vermicelli in a tangy tamarind gravy), beef or mutton *rendang* (a kind of Indonesian dry curry) with *nasi briyani*, and my great weakness, *epok epok*, the Malay-style half-moon-shaped curry puff filled with curried onion and sardine, or potato and egg, like a spicy pastie.

Then there was the Indian food stall, where you could get *roti prata* (known in South India as *roti paratha*, and in Malaysia as *roti canai*) with chicken, fish or vegetarian curry, Indian-style curry puffs (deep-fried, triangular, with a crunchy, flaky filo-like pastry, filled with potato and mutton curry), *tandoori* chicken with rice, and brightly coloured Indian sweets such as *barfi*, which is similar to the Australian coconut ice.

Across one end of the canteen was the drinks stall, where you would buy fizzy soft drinks, packaged ice creams, lollies and snacks like crisps, cotton candy, as well as Asian drinks like cold, sweetened chrysanthemum tea, barley water, lime juice, grass jelly, coconut juice with pulp, and *bandung*—a mix of rose syrup and evaporated milk. You could get a tiny packet of salty biscuits for ten cents, or an ice pop for twenty cents. At age seven, I had a whole dollar in pocket money, which increased to a dollar-fifty when I was nine, then two dollars when I was twelve. This was to be my first understanding of the concepts of wage increase and inflation.

When I went home after school in the early afternoon, I might have lunch with my grandfather, who loved to take me to eat at a food stall near our home. It sold minced pork and mushroom noodles, which was one of the last meals he asked for when he was home after major surgery for liver cancer. At home, I would ask him if he wanted a coffee. I loved making him coffee. I loved measuring out the instant coffee granules (Nescafé), spooning in the thick condensed milk, adding the scalding water from the thermos (the only time I was allowed to use it), and the sound of the teaspoon rattling against the glass. Or he might sit at the sofa in front of the TV and perform a tea ceremony. He would boil water in a small kettle on a hotplate right there on the coffee table, steep Chinese tea leaves in a little teapot, and serve tea in tiny handle-less cups on a bamboo tray.

My grandmother usually cooked the family dinner as my mother would still be at work. There would always be a clear soup (my favourite was winter melon soup with carrot, water chestnuts, mushrooms and chicken), a vegetable dish, a meat dish and at least one other dish, plus steamed white rice. One of my grandmother's specialities was deep fried fish fillets, which she would coat in a light batter seasoned with dried plum powder. This lent the fish an irresistible sweet-salty taste. The fillets would later be covered in a gravy, but I would try to sneak as many of the crisp morsels before I was yelled at to get out of the kitchen. Another of her Hokkien specialities is sliced pork belly braised in soy, served with steamed chinese buns, to be assembled at dinnertime—the only time I was allowed to use my hands to eat.

After I turned sixteen, I was allowed to date. The first boy I dated introduced me to curried instant noodles. It was his favourite after-school meal to make: curry-flavoured instant ramen noodles and a beaten egg was his idea of paradise. To this day, I cannot eat curried noodles without thinking of him.

My first serious relationship was with a young man whom I met in the early years of being an undergraduate at university. He loved *Indomie*—Indonesian instant noodles which would be drained and then covered in a sweet soy sauce (*kecap manis*) and chilli powder. He also loved to add cooked instant ramen noodles to a tin of Campbells' condensed soup, making a poor man's version of creamy pasta. I would cook him fried rice, and grill chicken wings for his friends when they gathered to play card games.

As I grew older, and dated more worldly men, the food I was introduced to became increasingly complex. One very charming suitor flew me to Bangkok for the weekend and took me to some beautiful places, including a modern Thai restaurant (where he ordered me a cocktail as well as champagne), an open-air fine dining bar/restaurant on the rooftop of a skyscraper, and a Michelin-starred Italian restaurant on the bank of the Chao Praya.

It's no surprise that the man I ended up with for nearly ten years was a serious foodie. Together, we ate our way through Singapore, Sydney, New York, San Francisco, London, Paris, and Rome. With him, I have been to many of the world's finest restaurants, and sampled the most interesting and inventive fare from some rather famous chefs. We threw uncountable memorable dinner parties at our home, where I learnt that to cook six courses for twelve people was an actual (if rather stressful) possibility.

After the end of that long relationship, I casually dated for some months. Over a meal of fish head curry in Singapore, my date, a chef who hailed from New York, asked me to name my favourite restaurant in NYC. 'Le Bernadin,' I'd replied. It turned out that he had been working in the kitchen there, possibly on the occasions I'd dined there. A man I hadn't even met yet then had cooked for me—and to me that was somehow more intimate, more fortuitous, than the fact that we were on a date at all.

Back in Sydney, I went on a couple of dates with an Englishman, but my interest waned when I realised that the man didn't bother to eat dinner, because he thought it wasn't necessary. What could we possibly have in common? A couple of friends then set me up with a mutual friend of theirs, whom I liked instantly, and connected with deeply over a Chinese meal. He told me that he had spent the last couple of weeks helping out in his friend's dad's Chinese restaurant in Canberra, and showed me his hands, raw from peeling vegetables all day in the kitchen.

Eventually, I met my husband, Colin. Our initial conversations were not about food. In fact, I tried to pretend that I didn't know how to cook, but he didn't believe me for an instant. We established early on that he was a huge fan of chilli, which I cannot do without. We don't have the money to eat out all the time, much less at fine dining establishments, but it doesn't really matter—we cook five or six nights a week, and nearly every meal we create is gourmet, by our (high) standards. We both like all the same food, which is nearly everything that is not fast food. We both believe in making simple food from fresh ingredients. Colin has skills that I don't, such as making pastry and bread, and the best béchamel sauce I have ever tasted. I have more time to shop and dream up recipes. Our greatest joy is in cooking together, and in consuming the results of our shared labour. You learn so much about someone by cooking alongside them, by watching the way they think, plan and work, by how they eat, and how they share cleaning up duties (the man is an obsessive cleaner, as I am).

I don't write a food blog, or post reviews of restaurants, but food comes through in so much of my poetry; it forms the background to so much of my work. Food, for me, is representative of family, culture, nourishment and love. I've learned how to cook from my grandmother, my mother, my friends' mothers, and my partners over the years. The dishes I prepare are a palimpsest of experiences and cultures, new and old. It's not good manners to kiss and tell, but no one said anything about eating and telling.

THE LONG HOURS POLISHING EACH DARK GRAIN INTO PEARLY WHITE

BURNING RICE

I did not mean to burn the rice tonight.
'Planting rice is never fun'—generations
of men, women and children ankle-deep
in padi fields, bent double at the waist,
immersing seedlings day after day.

Finally, the harvest: sharp scythes glinting
in the afternoon sun, stalks of ripened grain tossed
into baskets strapped onto backs like babies too young
to walk. Next, the rice huller, churning husks
away from the hearts. Then the long hours polishing

each dark grain into pearly white. I'd forgotten
that brown rice needed more than double
the usual measure of water. I smelt the charring,
then saw: scorched rice like black gold,
my ancestors' ashes in a bowl.

MID-AUTUMN MOONCAKES

It's nearly mid-autumn. I spy the tins
at the Asian grocer—gaudy red peonies
unchanged for forty years. Of course
I buy the mooncakes with double yolks:

here in Australia, yolk or no yolk,
they cost the same. I should wait for you,
wait for the full moon, light some lanterns
and try to make out the lunar rabbit,

the Chinese fairy, but I don't. I cut
the mooncake into quarters and spoon
out the deep orange yolks, leaving
half-round cavities in the sweet

lotus paste. Eaten on their own,
the yolks are creamy, almost too salty.
A continent away, my mother in her kitchen
would be slicing through shell

and briny white, my father would be scraping
duck eggs into rice porridge. They always saved me
the yolks. My bowl, a cradle of bright congee
full of the gold of the mid-autumn moon.

GRANDMOTHER'S DISH

Buy the freshest prawns, grey ones
are the sweetest. Peel them, tails and all,
and save the shells, especially the heads.

Use your biggest pot. Heat some oil, then fry
garlic, whole cloves, and spring onion tied
into a knot. Add the shells and fry until they

turn pink. Now the pork bones. Add water.
How much? Enough. You'll know. Bring to the boil
then let it simmer until the water turns red.

Pluck the tau gay tails, all of them. We can do it
together while we watch the Taiwanese drama.
Cook the pork belly strips in the stock

until they are firm enough to slice. Cut
the fishcake thinly, on an angle. Better that way.
Now the noodles: mix yellow and white. Fry

in the wok with garlic, add prawn, pork, fishcake,
fry some more, then add a little stock. Cover
and let it cook. Be patient. Good things must wait.

Add the tau gay, then crack the eggs into the dish and stir. Add pepper and salt now, but only white pepper from Indonesia. Angmoh pepper not nice.

Ask who wants to eat. Don't forget the sambal. How to make sambal? That's another dish. Today is Hokkien Prawn Mee. Eat now, while it's hot.

CHINESE GINSENG

> Go and catch a falling star,
> Get with child a mandrake root,
> Tell me where all past years are,
> Or who cleft the devil's foot
>   'Song', John Donne

'Try ginseng,' my mother says. 'Must be Chinese,
not Korean or American.' I remember the ginseng's
bulbous head, its desiccated torso, smaller roots

for arms and legs—bound with red string to cardboard backing,
displayed in boxes stacked for sale. Panacea, tonic, necessity.
The medicine man extols the virtues of each unique root,

then shaves the ginseng into slices so thin
I could melt them on my tongue. He weighs them
on a brass scale pinched between forefinger and thumb,

then wraps portions into paper packages. There is no point
in telling my mother what she doesn't want to hear: polycystic ovaries,
endometriosis, infertility. Instead, I just listen—I can almost taste

her soup: sweet dates and wolfberries, smoky angelica and lilybulb,
but above all, the unmistakable bitter-sweetness of Chinese ginseng.

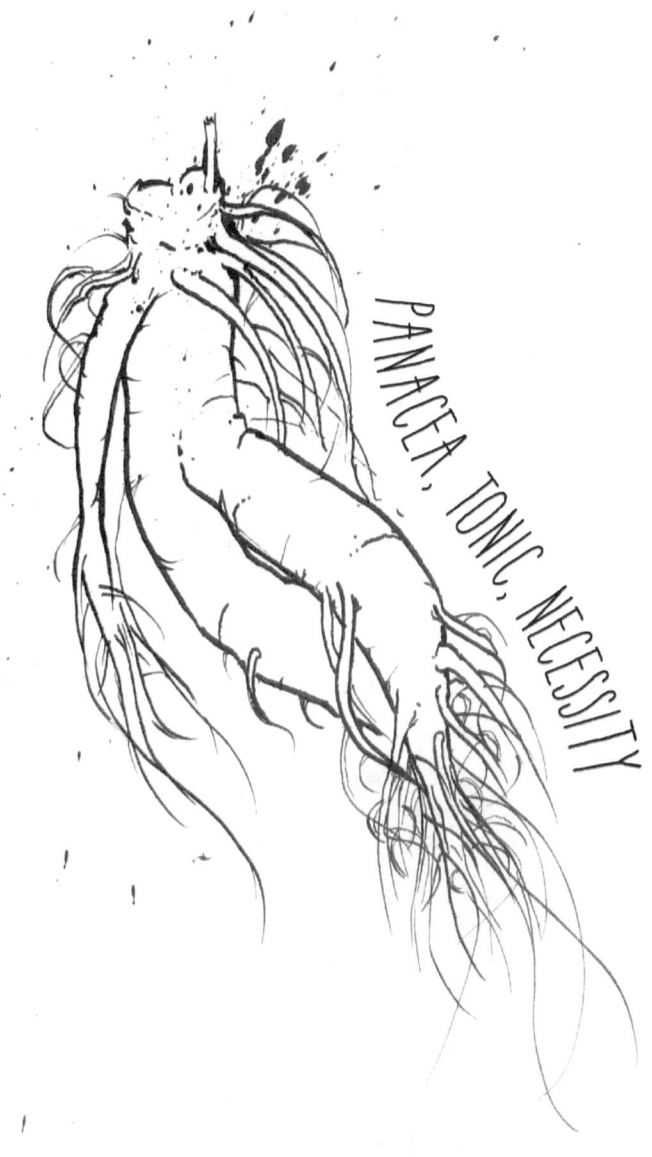

CHINESE GINSENG CHICKEN SOUP

serves 4

Ingredients:

One free range chicken, whole

1 litre salt reduced chicken stock

Two handfuls of dried shiitake mushrooms, whole or sliced

½ cup dried Chinese wolfberries (also known as goji seeds or goji berries)

½ cup sliced dried American ginseng

200 ml Chinese rice wine (shaoxing wine)

Method:

Place chicken, breast side down, in large heavy-bottomed pot.

Add all dried ingredients into pot, distributing evenly around chicken.

Add all liquid ingredients, making sure liquid rises to cover at least 3/4 of the chicken.

Cover and bring to the boil, then lower heat to simmer for about 1.5 hours.

When soup is done, remove the chicken from the pot, and let cool. Remove the skin, and separate the flesh from the bones.

Peel the flesh into bite-sized pieces. Discard the bones.

Skim excess fat off the top of the soup.

Add chicken meat back to the soup.

Season with pepper and salt if needed and serve.

CLEANSING RITUAL

My grandmother pinches the yellow charm
and sets it alight. The red writing shrivels
then curls onto the bottom of a mug. In a pot
on the stove, dried chrysanthemums unfurl

their secrets, truths hushed by rock sugar
then boiled into limp silence. Black and white ashes
float in tea. I drink it in one go, tasting shadows:
leached flowers, cane sap. I dip my hands

and feet in a bucket filled with blooms. She daubs
the holy water across my face before she weaves
a net of sandalwood smoke around me,
head to toe. This is exorcism, purification, love.

I realise I don't have the recipe, so I make it up as I go.
I write words on this page, and throw out the withered orchids.

EVENSONG

A poem is a heavy thing. It weighs
as you scrub the potatoes,
rub them with salt, then decide
to boil them instead. A poem
is a heavy thing. You carry its strain
as you lay plates on the table, as you set
out cutlery. A poem is
a heavy thing. Even the brownness
of the chicken's skin reminds you
of your grandfather's hands
in the dirt. Of his feet on the deck
when he caught the fish. A poem is a heavy
thing. You'd wanted greens
but instead bought beansprouts, pale
with their arching necks, tails intact
because you couldn't bear the smell
of your grandmother's hours
at the sink, plucking, washing, plucking.
A poem is a heavy thing.
When your husband comes
home from work, you think
man, labour, dust, evensong

as he kisses you and asks
how your day was. Heavy,
you tell him. Heavy.

FATHER, CROW

> this ink painting of wind blowing through pines
> who hears it?
>   'Crow with No Mouth: Ikkuyu',
>   versions by Stephen Berg

I see old men at the station,
on the bus, in the streets,
and I stumble. *My father*—

stooped, thin backs,
grey thatches of hair,
spindly legs, bowlegged.

They all look the same,
these Chinese men
dressed in identical jackets.

Watery eyes, lined faces.
Broken hands clutching
crumpled packages.

Inside the bag, a bowl
of soup my mother
cooked over a low fire.

Three portions: one for father,
one for mother, one for me.
Daughter, flown bird, grown self.

We are in a room filled
with the scent of pine ink.
Words dragged across paper

line the walls. My father
reads me the poems.
My mother is counting

the hours: to cut a chicken
into its parts, to boil water,
add dates, dried woodears,

rock sugar, a pinch of salt.
To simmer into broth.
What of the steam?

No one sees it
paint itself, drop by drop:
clouds ghost on glass.

EATING DURIAN

The knife in my father's hand.
A shallow incision; a careful prising
open, fingers fluttering with the effort.

We wait, greedy, knowing the taste
of the prize. Firm flesh, custard within.
We put the fruit to our mouths.

Our eyes roll back in pleasure.
Surely no one was meant for this.
King. Thorns. Stench.

AUGUST, POMELO

The pomelo is not a grapefruit.
My father tells me of the cashier
who did not know this. He unbags
his prize, smells it—ripe, sharp—

and hands it to me. It is heavy
in my palm, which means the fruit
is juicy. My father watches me
take the knife to the pomelo.

This is one of his lessons.
Decide where pith meets flesh.
Cut the top off. Make eight
evenly-spaced incisions all around

the curve. Drop the knife.
With your thumb, press firmly
into the pith, and prise it
from the flesh. Repeat.

Raw globe of naked fruit.
Crescent segments. Pinch at
the membrane, peel it apart.
Teardrop pearls, citrus heart.

POMELO, PORK AND PRAWN SALAD

Serves 4

Ingredients:
1 ripe pomelo, peeled (leave flesh in small chunks)
1 pork loin, lean
300 grams of prawns (cooked and peeled)
1 bunch chinese coriander, finely chopped
1 bunch thai basil, finely chopped
1 bunch mint, finely chopped
1 spanish onion, finely sliced
2 long red chillies, finely sliced
1 carrot, finely grated
1 cucumber, cut into chunks
1 handful raw beansprouts, rinsed
½ cup fried shallots

Dressing:
combine all ingredients below
1 tablespoon brown sugar (muscavado is best)
½ cup fish sauce
½ cup vinegar (rice or apple cider)
1 tablespoon sesame oil
Juice from ½ lime

Method:

Boil water in a pot, add pork loin and reduce to a simmer. Cover and cook pork loin until firm, about 10-15 minutes.

Rest the pork for 10 minutes, then slice and set aside.

In a large bowl, toss all ingredients except pomelo, prawn, pork and fried shallots, until just combined.

Place salad on a large serving platter or bowl, and arrange the pomelo pieces, pork and prawns on top.

Drizzle the dressing over the salad, paying special attention to the pork and prawns.

Top with fried shallots and serve.

MY MOTHER CHOSE CRABS AT THE MARKET

THE TASK

after Sharon Olds

My mother chose crabs
at the market. Grey-green armour,

impenetrable. The crabs would sit in a basin
on the floor of the laundry while she

pounded spices. I once filled the tub
with water. I'd thought they might drown.

In the sink, my mother would push aside
their legs, locate their underside flaps

and stab them with the pointed end
of a chopstick. I'd read that you could kill

crabs by placing them in the freezer. A slow,
painless death. It was my task to unwrap

the string from the dead ones. My father would
prise off their top shells, remove the gills,

and rinse out the guts. My mother quartered
each with a cleaver. When the crabs arrived

at the table, swimming in sauce, my father
would reassemble his. Lift the carapace.

I liked breaking off the legs, snapping the joints
and easing out the flesh in one sliver.

Biting the meat off the cartilage in a single
pull. I left the claws to the others,

preferring only what I could mine
through my own precise undoings.

SINGAPORE CHILLI CRAB

serves 4

Ingredients:

4 crabs, cleaned and quartered

(mud crabs are the best, but any crab will work, or you could substitute prawns with shell on)

8 garlic cloves, minced

½ onion, minced

One thumb-sized knob of ginger, finely minced

½ cup peanut or rice bran oil

1 cup tomato paste

4 tablespoons sweet chilli sauce (choose your spice level, I use a spicy garlic chilli sauce)

6 long red chillies, minced (leave seeds in for heat if desired)

1 litre chicken stock

2 eggs, beaten

2 tablespoons cornstarch

½ cup water

Garnish:

½ cup spring onions, chopped

½ cup coriander, chopped

Method:

Heat oil in a wok (wok must have a lid), or a large dutch oven.

When oil is very hot, add onions, garlic, ginger and chilli, and cook for about one minute.

Add crab and chicken stock, increase the heat and bring to a boil.

Lower the heat until liquid is simmering, and cover the wok or pot.

Check the crab after about five minutes; the shells should have turned red. The crabs are not fully cooked at this stage.

Remove the lid, add the tomato paste and the chilli sauce, simmer.

Season with salt and pepper, and add more chilli sauce if you want more spice.

Mix cornstarch in a small bowl with the water to form a paste.

Add cornstarch to the pot and stir well to thicken the sauce. Bring to the boil.

Turn the heat off, and stir in the beaten egg. Top with garnish and serve.

KUMERA

Wrap whole sweet potatoes,
skin on, in foil. Place among
the embers of coals—long after

the chicken wings and satay
have run out: the tender, orange
flesh of the kumera—steaming

in the night air, smoky skin
peeled off in strips. One winter,
in Kunming, ascending the path

to the Dragon's Gate, a woman
standing watch over an oil drum.
Scent of sweet potatoes cooking—

men devouring its meat by the roadside.
In the war it was all that would grow
in the gardens, fertilised by shit.

I ask my mother for rice porridge
boiled with kumera. This thin gruel:
the bright, cubed gifts of our survival.

COOKING FOR ONE

> I want to go home, I just want to go home, but this is where I live.
> 'Skyshow', Toby Davidson

Things you can cook for one: a bowl
of somen noodles. A single egg. Asparagus
salad with curled trout. Toasted almonds
fragrant with burning. Salt capers dancing

on your tongue. A plate of pasta, dressed
with oil, herbs, and cheese. Glistening blueberries
eaten with a spoon. Sandwiches, so many
sandwiches, clamped between fingertips,

leaving their grease on paper. This glass of wine,
this mug of tea, these leaves discarded after
scalding. You hold hands with yourself,
feeling your own pulse, the regular beats

stroking on. Time proceeds and carries buoyant
those dreams that leave you restless, turning
and seeking a face in the night. Things you cook
for one: contentment, quiet, and a small pot of hot congee.

RICE-DUMPLINGS

for Joyce Cutler

Bamboo leaves, scalded into olive greenness,
kept moist under a damp tea-towel. You marinated the pork
while I snipped the stems from shiitake, plump and juicy
from rehydration. Chestnuts we'd bought in a packet—here

there are no men on street corners churning them
in a wok over tarry coals. We peeled the shells
of salted duck eggs, discarding the chalky whites,
cutting bright yolks into eighths. We talked

of our mothers and their kitchens while we worked.
You chopped the shallots till you wept, wiping
your eyes on your sleeve. I laughed at your garlic
in a jar. Dried shrimp in the pan with oil, pungent

as old socks. Mung beans, washed until their green skins
slipped off. We rendered pork fat in a pan, then stir-fried
raw glutinous rice with five spice, oyster sauce, soy and sugar.
All the ingredients are ready: this is the part I came for. You hold up

three large leaves and fold them into a cone, then pack rice,
beans, meat, mushrooms, chestnuts and egg yolk into its cavity,
finishing with beans and rice. There's magic in the way you hold
the cone, in the movements of your fingers as they pinch

the top leaf over its contents, then fold and seal
the pyramid shut. We tie raffia around each dumpling
in circles, knotting it tight, careful to leave a long string
at the end. I make small ones for your daughter. Our legs ache

from standing all afternoon; our hands are tired. We use
your largest pot and put water onto the boil, then lower
the dumplings by their tails. It's reverse fishing. We clap
the lid on and wait. You make us cups of tea

and I cut you a slice of old-fashioned lemon drizzle cake.
What are we, if not old-fashioned? Reviving the art
of rice dumplings in an inner-city apartment in Sydney
five minutes' walk from Chinatown. An hour and more:

bamboo scents the room. We truss up the steaming parcels
and drain them in the sink. You unwrap one in a bowl. Look
how it glistens… We eat at the counter, murmuring our approval,
marveling at our true selves, so far, yet so close to home.

ASH, WEDNESDAY

Mid-autumn Festival, 2017

I pour tea from the pot I bought
twenty years ago, before I even
had a home. Our home is quiet

except for your tapping at the desk.
The old cat breathes audibly. I count
the bumps along his spine—he wakes,

purrs, then sinks back into sleep.
The spring herbs have been planted;
death has nourished the soil. Last night,

we hung lanterns from the trees, beneath
the brimming moon. One caught fire.
We watched it burn, until all became ash.

In the morning the sun rose, brighter
than salt. Cut deep. Sweetness of skin.

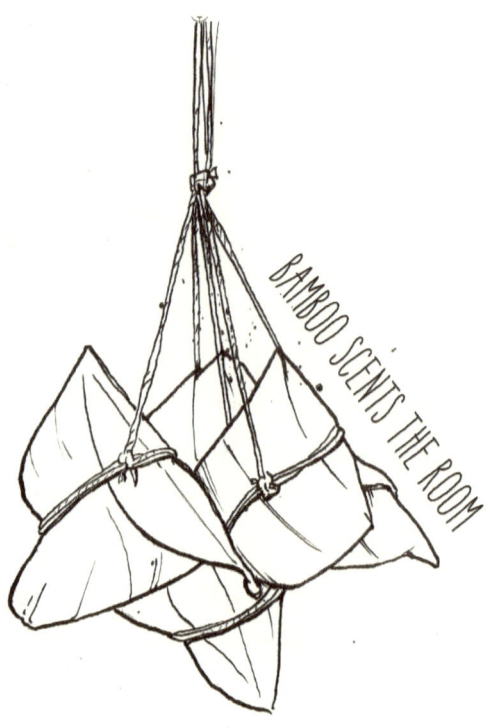

bamboo scents the room

SUN MING RESTAURANT, PARRAMATTA

> The noise the body makes
> when the body meets
> the soul over the soul's ocean and penumbra
> is the old sound of up-and-down, in-and-out
>
> 'The Cleaving', Li-Young Lee

My lover takes me to his favourite Chinese
restaurant, near his home. I came by train
from the inner city where I live, passing from
prostitutes and pimps, bikers in leather vests

and chains to the quiet faces of the suburbs.
In the carriage I meet two little girls speaking
in Mandarin. The elder holds the hand
of the younger, telling her not to be afraid.

My lover holds my hand and walks me through
an unfamiliar cityscape. I see the restaurant
from across the street: gleaming roast ducks,
golden soya chickens, juicy barbequed pork.

We cross the threshold into Hong Kong—
the cacophony of Cantonese, rich smells,
live fish in tanks. He's the only non-Asian there.
He tells me he used to forget he was a *gwei lo*

until he would notice people staring at him
as he ate his food. How did we find each other
in this faceless city, on this wide continent,
coming as we did from worlds so far apart?

I eat my congee with sliced pork liver
and a raw egg; he tucks into a bowl of noodles
with crisp duck on a plate. We share hot tea, spinach
with three kinds of egg, and learn a new rhythm.

XIAO LONG BAO (LITTLE DRAGON DUMPLINGS)

Behind the glass, men and women dressed like surgeons
(masks across their faces, hair tucked under caps)
roll out pastry into circles on a floured bench-top.

Cool hands: they cup the skin of each dumpling
in one palm then spoon a perfectly shaped
dollop of spiced pork into the middle

then deftly, invisibly, stretch the pastry and pinch
the top shut in a series of fan-folds. Sixteen creases
form the crest of each dumpling; eight dumplings

to a bamboo steamer lined with a cabbage leaf.
Circular trays stacked nine tall, straddling a wok
of boiling water, steamed for exactly eleven minutes.

Finely shredded young ginger topped
with black rice vinegar and a dash of soy
form the dipping sauce. I teach you

how to lift each dumpling carefully with chopsticks
into your Chinese spoon, to dress each morsel
with stained ginger, to bite through its skin with the tips

of your front teeth and suck out the hot soup
from the dumpling before placing it into your mouth.
I still remember the look on your face when you ate
your first little dragon dumpling. Sudden understanding.

LORD NELSON

The men crowd so close around
the bed bright with evanescent light—
his last words: *Kiss me, Hardy*. His friend

bent close and kissed him twice: first
on the cheek, then on the forehead,
tenderly, like a mother before

her child crosses over into the realm
of dream. Right eye and right arm lost
by the time of his death. One can only

imagine the blood and gore soaking
the orlop deck. Who lifted the body
into the barrel? Who filled the cavity

with brandy? Who sealed the lid? Who
moved the bloated corpse? Who drenched
it in wine? At the end, a pickled prune.

We hoist pints of Three Sheets at the pub.
The poet is shaking, spilling his beer.
Words carved into sandstone hold no spirit.

SUDDEN UNDERSTANDING

CROSSING THE SPEY

after Philip Levine's 'Letters to the Dead'

I cut the white ends off
the spring onions, scatter salt
onto the bottom of a bowl,
and save them for you.

It's a Cassidy thing, you said.
Your grandfather loved to eat
them. Your father does, too.
I mix the two up. Who played
the piano? Who was left for dead?

Or were they the same man?
Tonight, over dinner, you told me
a new story: how you crossed
a footbridge over the Spey

to a stone house on the edge
of a forest. You drank whisky
in front of a fire in the thick of winter.
Strange to think of your lives

without me: before me, after me.
I should like to see it for myself.
Gorse and heather. Glen and hill.
The snow falling clean in the gloaming.

A WINTER'S NIGHT

What would you like for dinner? I asked.
Scotch broth, he says. And so I peel potatoes,
parsnips and swedes; I chop onions, celery,
and leeks. I season and roast lamb shanks,
then add everything into a pot and cover it
with stock. Now to simmer for hours,
or as he said, to *Cook the hell out of it*. I read
that you'd give it a good stir at the end
to smash up the winter vegetables and thicken
the soup. I add three handfuls of pearl barley
an hour before the soup is ready. The meat
is falling off the bone and I cut it
into bite-sized pieces. By this time
he is on the train and will soon step out
into the cold night air towards home,
to an apartment smelling of lamb soup.
He will take his jacket off and hang it up
and bend to stroke the dozing cats
before holding me like I am something
precious and breakable. He will set the table
and pour us a drink each and sneak a taste
of the soup before exclaiming *Braw!*
When we sit down to eat he speaks
of his grandmother's Scotch broth

and tells me he feels like he is in Scotland.

This, here, made from my hands,

his memories—we consume spoon after spoon

of history and desire and laugh about the future.

EILEEN'S SCOTCH BROTH

Serves 4

Ingredients:

2 litres beef stock, or water

Leftover lamb roast (make sure there's plenty of meat left on the bone), or 4 lamb shanks

1 onion, cut into chunks

2 swedes, peeled and cut into chunks

2 turnips, peeled and cut into chunks

2 carrots, peeled and cut into chunks

4 medium potatoes, peeled and cut into chunks

1 cup pearl barley, rinsed

Bouquet garni

Salt and pepper

Method:

If using uncooked lamb shanks, season with salt and pepper, drizzle with olive oil, and roast in a moderately hot oven (180 degrees celcius) for 25 minutes.

Heat oil in a large pot, and add onions. Cook until translucent (do not brown).

Add carrots, potatoes, swedes and turnips. Cook for about 5 minutes.

Add lamb, stock or water, and herbs to the pot. Lid and bring to the boil.

Lower the heat to allow the soup to simmer. Add barley.

Simmer the soup for as long as is possible; minimum 1 hour. Stir from time to time.

Before you serve the soup, stir it hard so as to smash up the vegetables and thicken the broth.

Season and serve. As with many soups and stews, the flavour continues to develop and the soup is even better the following day.

AFTERWORD

I write a lot about food. Like many people in Singapore, I am a little food obsessed. There is a real culture around eating in Singapore —especially around eating out. There were street hawkers from before 1960, which evolved into contained, sheltered spaces called 'hawker centres'. This was the precursor to the air-conditioned food court of today. It's very cheap to eat out in Singapore, although this is changing. When I was growing up in the 1980s, you could get a bowl of noodles at the hawker centre for SGD1.50. Today it's more like SGD3 to 4, but comparative to Australia, it's still very cheap. My maternal grandmother was a hawker—she cooked a dish called 'fried hokkien prawn noodles' at the Albert Complex near Chinatown. She raised six children with her earnings from this, and from other jobs.

I wrote a poem called 'Grandmother's Dish', which is in *Burning Rice*. I didn't intend to turn the recipe into a poem, but I did. I was missing my grandmother and this dish, which is often cooked at family gatherings. The poem is written in tercets, and its rhythm is quite staccato, which echoes the Hokkien speech patterns of my grandmother. It is a kind of running commentary-recipe that takes place across cultures. I was sitting in a café in Potts Point a few weeks ago and there were two women friends next to me having coffee. The bulk of their conversation was made up of the sharing of a recipe for pea and ham soup. One of the women, who was Asian, insisted that her pea and ham soup, made without the use of split peas, but with fresh peas, tastes better. I enjoyed eavesdropping on the sharing of this recipe, which revealed so much about the meeting of cultures and preferences.

Cooking is a creative act, like writing poetry. There is a tradition of poems about food, about the preparing of it, the sharing of it, that I am drawing on. I am thinking of Li-Young Lee's marvellous food poems, in particular the poems on persimmons, as well as the dyad 'Eating Alone' and 'Eating Together', Sharon Olds' 'Crab', Mark Strand's 'Coming to This', Andy Kissane's 'Meat Matters'… there are so many others. Gastronomic poetry is wonderful. I have written about Chinese mooncakes, *xiao long bao*, rice-dumplings, Hokkien prawn noodles of course… Congee is one of my comfort foods and is a bit of a personal symbol for me. And my first book is called *Burning Rice*! Things like mussels, bagels, lemon drizzle cake also make brief appearance in poems. In my third book I also have a poem about Scotch broth, which is a very new dish to me. It's a dish from Scotland, a stew-like soup made with lamb and barley and winter root vegetables like swede and turnip. It's the comfort food of my partner, who is Scottish. I think that one acquires recipes and foods through people and experiences in a way one might acquire history and culture. It's about sharing, assimilation, translation, recreation, and nourishment.

NOTES

'Burning Rice': the line 'planting rice is never fun' is taken from the folk song, 'Planting Rice'.

'Lord Nelson': The poem references the British naval hero, Horatio Nelson (29 September 1758–21 October 1805), also known as Lord Nelson; *The Death of Nelson*, a painting of Lord Nelson's death at the Battle of Trafalgar aboard the HMS *Victory* by Arthur Devis; as well as the brewery and pub in The Rocks in Sydney that bears his name.

After his death, Lord Nelson's body was first preserved in a cask of brandy, stored upright. Upon HMS *Victory*'s arrival in Gibraltar, the body was transferred to a lead-lined coffin and preserved in spirits of wine. The HMS *Pickle*, a topsail schooner, was the first ship to bring news of Lord Nelson's victory at Trafalgar back to England, as well as the news of his death. 'Three Sheets' is the name of the signature beer of the *Lord Nelson*.

ACKNOWLEDGEMENTS

'The Common Table' was first published in *Meanjin* on 8 December 2017, at https://meanjin.com.au/blog/the-common-table/ (last accessed 13 December 2017).

'Diana's Hainanese Chicken Rice' was written in conjunction with Diana Lim Hong Hua on 24 January 2017.

'Eating and Telling: A Personal Food History' was first published in *Southerly Journal* on 4 July 2016 at http://southerlyjournal.com.au/2016/07/04/eating-and-telling-a-personal-food-history/ (last accessed 13 December 2017).

'Burning Rice', 'Mid-autumn Mooncakes', 'Grandmother's Dish', and 'Chinese Ginseng' were published in *Burning Rice*, (2012), Pitt Street Poetry, Sydney, Australia.

'Cleansing Ritual', 'Rice-dumplings', and 'Evensong' were published in *Peony*, (2014), Pitt Street Poetry, Sydney, Australia.

'Cooking for One', 'Xiao Long Bao (Little Dragon Dumplings)', 'Sun Ming Restaurant, Parramatta', and 'A Winter's Night' were published in *Painting Red Orchids*, (2016), Pitt Street Poetry, Sydney, Australia.

'Father, Crow' was published in *Rambutan Literary Review,* Issue 4, at http://www.rambutanliterary.com/issue-four-eileen-chong.html (last accessed 13 December 2017).

'August, Pomelo', and 'Kumera' were published in *Peril Magazine*, Edition 30: Work Werk Work, on 25 May 2017, at http://peril.com.au/back-editions/work-werk-work/tide-other-poems/ (last accessed 13 December 2017).

'The Task' was published in *Overland* 228, Spring 2017.

My deep and abiding gratitude goes to:

Shane Strange of Recent Work Press for the wonderful idea of *The Uncommon Feast*, Judith Beveridge for writing the generous introduction to the book, Colin Cassidy for the beautiful cover design and inspired hand illustrations, and John and Linsay Knight of Pitt Street Poetry for their support of this project.

I have not forgotten my Home Economics teacher, Miss Leong, who in 1993, taught me to how to cook chicken congee; and my grandfather, Lim Choon Hoe, who ate my first independently cooked meal with great relish. Aunty Regina Wong, who was the most accomplished home cook I knew in 1991, for cooking me countless gourmet meals. Aunty Luan Koh, who went to so much trouble to cook Peranakan feasts for me, including my favourite, the labour-intensive bakwan kepeting.

All the men and women who have cooked for me, in kitchens commercial and domestic, large and small, throughout the world, I thank you. My grandmothers, Chin Koi Foh and Yeap Ah Choo, and my mother, Diana Lim, who have nurtured me in ways that went far beyond food. And once again, to my husband, Colin, the best cook I know, for sharing all that he has with me, in food, love and life.

Eileen Chong is a Sydney poet who was born in Singapore. Her books are *Burning Rice* (2012), *Peony* (2014), *Painting Red Orchids* (2016), and *Rainforest* (2018), all from Pitt Street Poetry. Her work has shortlisted for numerous prizes, including the Anne Elder Award, the Victorian Premier's Literary Award, and twice for the Prime Minister's Literary Awards. *Another Language* (2017) is published by George Braziller, New York, in the Braziller Series of Australian Poets, with a foreword by Paul Kane. www.eileenchong.com.au

2018 Editions

The Uncommon Feast **Eileen Chong**
Inlandia **Kerry Nelson**
Peripheral Vision **Martin Dolan**
The Love of the Sun **Matt Hetherington**
Things I Have Thought to Tell You Since I Saw You Last **Penelope Layland**
Moving Targets **Jen Webb**
The Many Uses of Mint **Ravi Shankar**
Abstractions **Various**

2017 Editions

A Song, the World to Come **Miranda Lello**
Cities: Ten Poets, Ten Cities **Various**
The Bulmer Murder **Paul Munden**
Dew and Broken Glass **Penny Drysdale**
Members Only **Melinda Smith** and **Caren Florance**
the future, un-imagine **Angela Gardner** and **Caren Florance**
Proof **Maggie Shapley**
Black Tulips **Moya Pacey**
Soap **Charlotte Guest**
Isolator **Monica Carroll**
Ikaros **Paul Hetherington**
Work & Play **Owen Bullock**

all titles available from
www.recentworkpress.com

www.ingramcontent.com/pod-product-compliance
Lightning Source LLC
Chambersburg PA
CBHW032049290426
44110CB00012B/1010